...Jansangharsh!

Satyameva Jayate...!

Keshav Mishra

<u>Contents</u>

<u>Contents below aren't a part of this book, they will be published in further volumes.</u>

- 4 Analyzing if an actual democracy even exists and if no then why?

- 5 Glory of Indian Democracy and comparison with other governments

- 6 Indian democracy from international standards

- 7 Constitution : A savior!

Keshav Mishra

- 8 Loopholes!

- 9 Constitutional rights and favors come with duties and responsibilities.

- 10 Point of views - An Individual, Poor, Rich, middle class, In power, without power etc.

- 11 Necessary changes

- 12 Can the utopia be changed into reality?

(Note : A brief description of each Chapter is provided in the synopsis)

Keshav Mishra

Keshav Mishra

<u>SYNOPSIS</u>

"India is not merely the world's democracy, India is the Mother of democracy. Our nation's temperament is democracy."

Current Prime Minister of India, Narendra Modi said those lines at the celebration of 75 years of independence while addressing the country. He deeply emphasized that India is the mother of democracy, a place where what we today see as modern democracy was birthed. India, when talking about world's polity is often referred to as the world's largest democracy. The world's largest democracy, it not only states that India is a democratic country with the highest population but also is homage to the faith of diversity in every kind. We can see diverse people based on religion, caste, race, sex, language, natural diversities like natives of mountains, plateaus, shores, plains, deserts, forests, islands etc. but during the critical time when nation is in danger, those people forget about their differences or bad blood to contribute the nation. Similarly, during votings, there are myriads of differences in opinions but most people still have their faith in the representative that is finally elected. In India, even after widest diversities people are still united and have faith in the democratic rule, their rule!

In India, we have an ancient legacy even from the pre-vedic times, we find many references that suggest the existence of democracy with a different name. In Rig Veda, we find many terms that indicate the elected representatives existed at that time. Furthermore, when King Dashrath had the of passing down his throne to Lord Ram, there were mentionings of an assembly.

After an excavation of Indus valley civilization and Harrapan civilization by Haryana Archaeological Department and Deccan College, Pune, many indirect signs indicate that the place wasn't ruled by a King or a Queen. It's most likely that democracy was the type of government that existed there.

Another shocking discovery indicated that in an inscription found while excavating the sites of chola dynasty at Uttaramerur in Kanchipuram district, many details about the rules of elections were found. It stated the criterias to become an representative of the village and the traces of a village assembly hall were found.

Keshav Mishra

Chanakya, in his Arthashastra mentioned how a King should welfare the people. His ideology coincides with what Wolpert termed as 'Social-Monarchy'. It wasn't a pure democracy but in the reign of Chandragupta at Mauryan Empire, traces were found about how he took advice and had direct dialogues with the public.

We will have a detailed discussion about all the aforementioned topics about our legacy of democracy from ancient India in chapter 1.

People say that there is a difference in the mindset of successful people, here we will take famous quotes from all over the globe and analyze if those are what we get or expect from democracy in India. We will see what is the most important aspect or the necessity of democracy, necessity in the democracy from their point of view in chapter 2.

Theories are just on paper, to practically put it into the ground, some newfound problems will arise and new solutions have to be sought for. Quoting what an ideal democracy would be isn't completely a great thing. To create what we think of as an ideal democracy, understanding every point of view in society is a must

Keshav Mishra

and having different personalities to get a wider perspective isn't an achievement, but a disease.

So we will dive into the world of fiction and build up a world from scratch according to all of the ancient and modern sayings and explore it. Here we'll be able to clearly find many loopholes in what we thought of as an ideal democracy, there may be monsters like corruption, selfishness, money, greed and a whole tribe full of them. We'll see how agents like corruption are the building blocks at the backstage of democracy. What will happen if no one is corrupted? (chapter 3)

If there is no other weapon to kill those monsters other than the nuclear weapon that is dictatorship then how do we even expect that a perfect democracy can exist. Is this whole term 'DEMOCRACY' just an utopia or can it be found in any corner of the world. We will have an epic battle between the conflicting thoughts, whether democracy exists or not in the 4th Chapter.

After having a tour all around the world searching for a perfect democracy, we'll finally return back to our India and realize that it is not as bad as it seems. There's a saying 'lesser evil is always good' and the same applies in the context. We will see how

Keshav Mishra

glorific the system of administration in India is despite it being the world's largest democracy from ancient times till now. (Chapter 5 and 6)

There are many instances where the elected representative himself gets stuck or strays off the path of a leader and the public starts suffering between the five years of him. This is the moment an angel-like figure descends, The Constitution of India. It equally provides the citizens their rights and freedom, for it, there is no difference between a road side vendor and the president. It is the most prominent figure in keeping all the high level officials in check and prevents the misuse or gathering of power in one hand. We will have a review of how the constitution is the savior of Indian democracy and it would be difficult to uphold the integrity of democracy without the support of constitution names pillar. (chapter 7)

Constitution is made by humans and humans make mistakes, for instance we may find many loopholes in constitution that are used by officials starting from a police constable, reaching as high as it could to their own use. In this segment, we will see the consequences of filling those loopholes. Will there be any ill effects of closing those loopholes, they are intentional? Or do the

Keshav Mishra

high ranking officials are tilted towards their own favor in opposition to public welfare? (Chapter 8)

But the Constitution isn't a god of power. It provides us with our six constitutional rights *(Right to equality, Right to freedom, Right against exploitation, Right to freedom of religion, Cultural and educational rights, Right to constitutional remedies.)* and six constitutional freedoms *(freedom of speech and expression, freedom of assembly without arms, freedom of association, freedom of movement throughout the territory of our country, freedom to reside and settle in any part of the country of India and the freedom to practice any profession.)* but asks us for the fundamental duties of citizens in return because these are the source of its power by which it can make the country function properly. The following are the eleven fundamental duties which every citizen must abide by

1. *Abide by the Constitution and respect national flag & National Anthem*
2. *Follow ideals of the freedom struggle*
3. *Protect sovereignty & integrity of India*
4. *Defend the country and render national services when called upon*

Keshav Mishra

5. Sprit of common brotherhood

6. Preserve composite culture

7. Preserve natural environment

8. Develop scientific temper

9. Safeguard public property

10.Strive for excellence

11.Duty of all parents/guardians to send their children in the age group of 6-14 years to school.

Now we will discuss the viewpoint of the most important pillars of Indian democracy like the poor, officials, women, youth, rich and even minors at length and try to understand what they want from the government. (Chapter 10)

Changes are part of human life. People change, their mindset changes, their values change, their needs change, everything changes with time and the same should apply to the way of administration. The coronavirus forced everyone to change and adapt to it. Schools were shutted down, offices were closed and factories were locked and from it we learned a new concept of work from home and India advanced towards digitalisation. Nowadays people prefer to use the unified payments portal in their mobile to pay their bills instead of old fashioned cash exchange. Similarly, a few changes in ways of administration will

Keshav Mishra

be proposed here in favor of every aspect of society or bring equality. (Chapter 11)

At last we will discuss if the utopia we talked about previously can be changed into reality and if yes then what will be the necessary steps to take by the government, executive board, judiciary, and most importantly, us the citizens of the Republic of India! (Chapter 12)

The debate on democratic values in the modern sense is Older than the American Revolution, however it gained real global attention during the revolution of 1789 in France when the in-house struggle shook the Imperial head of state and people's rule was established. A tyrannical legacy of imperial rulers and conquest of Kings and Dynasties across the world crushed the human values and social cohesiveness on multiple discriminatory grounds like religion, dialects, race, color, caste, nation, gender and wealth.

"The servants of the Company forced the natives to buy dear

Keshav Mishra

and sell cheap... Enormous fortunes were thus rapidly accumulated

at Calcutta, while thirty millions of human beings were reduced

to the extremity of wretchedness. They had never [had to live]

under tyranny like this...

—Macaulay"

"The government has converted the entire nation into a prison

and we are all prisoners. Going to prison only means that from

a big cell one is confined to a smaller one.

Bal Gangadhar Tilak"

As the suppression of "subject" went beyond the patience of united people, there came a revolution which not only uprooted their imperial masters but also spread the democratic debate to other colonies. Coupled with the world war, the struggle for democracy has the advantage of economic weakening of monastic rulers. The appetite for self governance and independence brought the commons under one roof and made them united.

Keshav Mishra

The varied perception of democracy among the leaders of the past led to the dynamic debate on the functioning and structure of democratization even after the adoption of a voted constitution in various nations and institutions.

"any claim for the sharing of power by the minority...[is] called communalism while the monopolising of the whole power by the majority...[is] called Nationalism.

—B.R. Ambedkar"

In the eyes of Dr Ambedkar, democracy indeed was the ropeway for the depressed and backward portion of society. The democratic ideas were minority centric and against the basic theme of majority's choice. This perception gave birth to many struggles between the majority and minority which literally stabbed in the dream of cohesive society in a democratic nation. Adding the political will to the simple notion of majority rule in democracy, the result is so complex with exploitation of citizens that the debates for prevention of social evil like corruption and

Keshav Mishra

hate speech are never summarized. However, a well defined constitution is strong enough to withstand such societal fluctuations and hold together all its citizens like the Indian constitution.

"I understand democracy as something that gives the weak the same chance as the strong." -

M K Gandhi"

Mahatma Gandhi was for such a stateless society in which life becomes perfect. People, without any prejudice, never become hindrance to one-other's routines. Moreover, self-regulation, self-dependency and mutual cooperation on priority become essential in day-to-day human practices. For Gandhi, the institution like the State or the system like democracy cannot be the final ideal. These institutions are based on political power, therefore, they can only be the means of enabling people to better their condition at different levels in different walks of life, but cannot lead human

Keshav Mishra

beings to achieve the goal of life. In this regard he clearly wrote in Young India on July 2, 1931, "To me political power is not an end but one of the means of enabling people to better their condition in every department of life. Political power means capacity to regulate national life through national representatives. If national life becomes so perfect as to become self-regulated, no representation becomes necessary. There is then a state of enlightened anarchy. In such a State everyone is his own master. He rules himself in such a manner that he is never a hindrance to his neighbor. In the ideal State, therefore, there is no political power because there is no State. But the ideal is never fully realized in life. Hence the classical statement of Thoreau that the government is best which governs the least is worthy of consideration."

In his own words, "There is no human institution but it has its dangers. The greater the institution the greater the chances of abuse. Democracy is a great institution and therefore it is liable

Keshav Mishra

to be greatly abused. The remedy, therefore, is not avoidance of democracy but reduction of possibility of abuse to a minimum." [Young India, May 7, 1931].

Mahatma Gandhi laid a great stress on decentralization of power so that participation of each and everyone in political and economic fields could ascertain. Moreover, on the strength of this participation common men could also enjoy a standard of living, and along with intellectual growth they could find a way to achieve equality in society.

"Democracy is an impossible thing until the power is shared by all..Even a pariah, a laborer, who makes it possible for you to earn your living, will have his share in self-government - Swarajya or democracy." [Young India, December 1, 1927]

Even in democracy many times we observe great lack in protecting and honouring the rights of citizens. More care for rights of self and less for others is noticed. Consequently, state of

Keshav Mishra

violation of human rights emerges time and again. For, undoubtedly, democracy suffers; its way gets obstructed. Therefore, Gandhi's view of connecting rights to duties cannot be undervalued. Rather, his ideas are important and worth consideration. They seem essential for the prosperity and success of people's government. In this regards his statement, "..if leaving duties unperformed we run after rights, they escape us like a will-o'-the-wisp" [Yong India, January 1, 1925] is extraordinary. Instead of overlooking, it makes the state of fundamental rights precious.

Hence, without a doubt, in democracy of Gandhi's imagination fundamental rights are as important as freedom and justice. Besides, his views regarding rights of citizens in democracy are worthy of consideration for subject specialist and those in the government. In their refined form they are also more or less capable in guiding those who are concerned of human rights.

Keshav Mishra

Apart from theorizing <u>different forms of democracy</u> the intellectuals and academicians structured the democratic nation on the pillars of elected legislature, regulated executives and guardian judiciary. Being the guardian in constitutional democracy, the interpretations and views of the judiciary on democratic values, ideas and doctrines is implicitly noteworthy and important for day to day business of democratic systems that make the human life dignified as well as protected. With the promulgation of evolving- judgments in various citizen centric cases, the constitutional benches have always reinforced the people's faith in democratic society and checked the breach of citizens rights. Landmark judgements like Golaknath case, Keshvanada Bharti Case, Indira Gandhi case, Maneka Gandhi case, Minerva Mills case, Puttaswamy case, Sabrimala Case to name a few.

Ours is a democracy with a written Constitution. We have a vibrant Legislature, Executive and Judiciary. Framers of our

Constitution should have kept in mind the sane advice of French political philosopher Montesquieu who was best known for The Spirit of Laws (1748), one of the great works in the history of political theory and of jurisprudence.

They postulated that concentration of power in one person or a group of persons results in tyranny. And, therefore, for decentralization of power to check arbitrariness, they felt the need for vesting governmental power in three different organs — the Legislature, the Executive, and the Judiciary.

This arrangement is well accepted by all the wings of democracy and more emphatically by the judiciary. In Sidheswar Sahakari Sakhar Karkhana Ltd vs. Union of India, the Supreme Court ruled,

"...Normally in such policy matters, a court of law will not interfere unless the policy is shown to be contrary to law,

inconsistent with the provisions of the Constitution or otherwise arbitrary or unreasonable."

No doubt the judiciary has a primary role in ensuring adherence to the rule of law. If any law is unconstitutional, the court can strike it down. If the court wanted to hear the government on this, it could have kept the laws in abeyance and served a notice to the government for further adjudication.

However, a rare practice of overreach and activism is also seen in the pillars of democracy. Consequent upon this, we find again ourselves in mid of turmoil of debate of democracy and inherited "Jansangharsh".

Keshav Mishra

CHAPTER - 1

"सं-समिद युवसे वर्षन्नग्रे विश्वान्यर्य आ |
इळस पदेसमिध्यसे स नो वसून्या भर ||
सं गछध्वं सं वदध्वं सं वो मनांसि जानताम |
देवा भागं यथा पूर्वे संजानाना उपासते ||
समानो मन्त्रः समितिः समानी समानं मनः सह चित्तमेषाम |
समानं मन्त्रमभि मण्त्रये वः समानेन वोहविषा जुहोमि ||
समानी व आकूतिः समाना हर्दयानि वः |
समानमस्तु वोमनो यथा वः सुसहासति ||"

"*THOU, mighty Agni, gatherest up all that is precious for thy friend. Bring us all treasures as thou art enkindled in libation's place.*

Assemble, speak together: let your minds be all of one accord, As ancient Gods unanimous sit down to their appointed share.

The place is common, common the assembly, common the mind, so be their thought united. A common purpose do I lay before you, and worship with your general oblation.

One and the same be your resolve, and be your minds of one accord. United be the thoughts of all that all may happily agree."

Keshav Mishra

Stated in Rig Veda, a sacred text, that forementioned *shloka* was to be sung in unison at the beginning of republican assembly in Ancient Times. To prefer a common assembly, common mind and common thought… over the tyrannical rule of King or Queen proves to an extent that there was democratic system in pre-vedic times. The Rig Veda is so committed towards democracy that it described democracy as a deity with name Samjnana which meant collective consciousness of people to which every individual pays its homage to.

The hymn addressed to Samjnana (in Rig Veda) called upon the people to gather in their assembly (*Samgachchaddhvam*) and speak there in one voice (*Samvadaddhvam*), in a union of minds (Sammanah), of hearts (*Samachittam*), of policy (*Samanmantrah*), and of hopes and aspirations (*akuti*).

However, rather than a few terms, which are mentioned in vedic texts, not much of a historical evidence is available to study and infer about democratic and republican system of ruling of that time. Many references state the following terms which gives a broad idea of what the government looked like at that time.

Keshav Mishra

Sabha - It was similar to the present times Lok Sabha and Rajya Sabha where the elders of the community attended the meetings. The pastoral issues were discussed and administrative actions were taken. Furthermore, the same assembly also exercised judicial powers which is contrastive to our current system of balance of power. The unique point is, in contrast to the other foreign historical records, women, who were called sabhavati were allowed to attend the assembly during the pre-vedic times (2800 to 1900 B.C.).

Samiti - The term came into light within the latest books of Rig Veda, which suggests that it assumed importance during the last stage of pre-vedic period. Rather than administrative or judicial meetings, this assembly shedded light on transactions and tribal business and focused on philosophical discussions and religious meetings with prayers. Many references suggest that the rajan was elected in this assembly.

Rajan - It was a person unanimously elected by the people as references suggest in samiti. It wasn't a permanent position and could be re-elected in Samiti in case of difference of opinion in public or retirement of rajan.

Later, the sabha became a small aristocratic body and the samiti ceased to exist indicating the arrival of monarchy.

Democracy in pre-vedic times was taken as inner unity and oneness in mindset of people and the policy governed the Indian Polity through ages and era either in foreground or background , directly or indirectly and landed back of the modified version of democracy. Thus, democracy existed since ancient times till the modern date in India, doesn't matter the form.

बेगि बिलंबु न करिअ नृप साजिअ <u>सबुइ समाजु</u>।
सुदिन सुमंगलु तबहिं जब रामु होहिं जुबराजु॥4॥

O king, let there be no delay, and make every preparation quickly. That day itself is auspicious and full of blessings, when Råma is proclaimed regent.

मुदित महीपति मंदिर आए। <u>सेवक सचिव सुमंत्रु बोलाए</u>॥
कहि जयजीव सीस तिन्ह नाए। भूप सुमंगल बचन सुनाए॥1॥

Keshav Mishra

The king returned rejoicing to his palace and summoned his servants and counselors including Sumantra. They bowed their heads saying, Victory to you may you live long! and the king placed before them the most auspicious proposal.

जौं पाँचहि मत लागै नीका। करहु हरषि हियँ रामहि टीका॥२॥

If this proposal finds favor with you all, install Råma on the throne with a cheerful heart.

Mentioned in ramcharitmanas that when King Dashrath wanted to pass down his throne to his son, Lord Ram, he met the *raj guru* and discussed the issue. He told the King not to delay any further and call the <u>public</u> to ask for opinions. With joy in heart, the king came back to the palace and summoned all of his ministers, officials, servants and the common people. After settling them down, he brought up the topic of passing the throne to lord Ram. He said "If you all agree to the proposal of making Ram the king, then please offer your blessings and make him the same."

It's crisp and clear that even if there was monarchy and the royal son was the heir of the kingdom, still, King Dashrath resolved to the opinion of the common public unlike that of usual

Keshav Mishra

monarchical practice. He was an ideal king that worked with keeping the public regardless of socio-economic differences in mind and opposed enforcing anything on people due to his own profit or greed. Thus, there is striking evidence that there was democracy, just not in name during King Dashrath's reign.

Indus valley civilization and the Harappan civilization are the few of the most famous civilisations of the past where people lived an organized life.

After the two year excavation of the over 550 hectares wide area of an ancient Harappan site in Hisar's Rakhigarhi village by the Haryana Archaeological Department and Deccan College, Pune, Traces of democratic rule were revealed. Furthermore, excavations pointed out that the panchayat system is over 5000 years old.

Prof Vasant Shinde, Vice-Chancellor, Deccan College, stated that there was no evidence found of a king's rule like that of those in Egypt and Mesopotamia in Harappan civilisation throughout the Asian subcontinent.

Keshav Mishra

"There are striking similarities in the lifestyle and socio-cultural behavior of people of Indus Valley Civilisation and that of modern civilisation. The study has revealed that Haryana people are descendents of Harappan people. Walking in present-day Rakhigarhi gives an impression that we are in a Harappan village," the VC said.

There is a major difference in lifestyle of people under different rules, democratic and monarchy/dictatorship. In the latter, slavery and events of protest are a few commons while on the other hand a gathering of assembly or elders to discuss an administrative or judicial issue is a common event in latter. A palace or similar infrastructure is kind of a must in the latter while an assembly hall or a similar thing is a must in the former.

"We found no palace-like structure or evidence of a rule of a king anywhere in Harappan sites. Unlike Egypt, people of Indus civilization did not waste their resources and forced common people to create structures such as pyramids which symbolize slavery," said Arvind Prabhakar Jamkhedkar, Chancellor, Deccan College.

Keshav Mishra

If the valuable resources were not wasted in the creation of symbols of slavery and people were valued then there is a large possibility that there was a system similar to democracy. Furthermore, the civilization was not the type of a primitive or barbaric. The city planning and infrastructure development with cross-bricks and drainage system indicates that the society was a high level one and it further enforces the idea that democracy existed in that time. Although there are not much direct evidences that will prove the existence of democracy, making a rough idea that leads to proving it with the help of supporting evidences isn't much of a difficult task.

If we take a peek at the southern part of India, we find that at Uttaramerur in Kanchipuram district there is an inscription that is from around 920 A.D. in the reign of Parantaka Chola [907-955 A.D.]. The inscription testifies to the historical fact that an insignificant village in the Chola dynasty had a refined and elaborated electoral system. A proper constitution was inscribed on a rectangular structure of the granite slabs that detailed about the mode of elections and village democracy.

Keshav Mishra

Astonishing details about the electoral system were revealed as Dr. Nagaswamy mentioned in his book. Constitution of wards, the qualification of candidates standing for elections, the disqualification norms, the mode of election, the constitution of committees with elected members, the functions of those committees, the power to remove the wrongdoer was vividly descriptive in Tamil.

On the rectangular structure, many transactive records were found. Furthermore, description of administrative as well as judicial dealings were found with records of commercial, agricultural, transportation and irrigation issues and regulations.

Most importantly, the people had the right to re-elect the representative if he failed his duty or dissatisfied the public.

Many Scholars believe that village assemblies might have existed even before the reign of Parantaka Chola but it was during his time that the village administration was honed and flourished into an evolved electoral system.

According to R. Sivanandam, epigraphist at the Tamil Nadu Department of Archaeology, there are many places in Tamil Nadu

Keshav Mishra

which mentions or hints the village assemblies but Uttaramerur had the earliest inscription which gave a complete sketch of what was the electoral system that time, what laws governed it and how does a new representative was elected.

R. Vasanthakalyani, retired chief epigraphist-cum-instructor at the department said that excluding the sick and those who have gone for pilgrimage, everyone including the infants had to present during village assemblies and elections.

Another point on which Dr. Nagaswamy emphasized, "The village assembly of Uttaramerur, drafted the constitution for the elections. The salient features were as follows: the village was divided into 30 wards, one representative elected for each. Specific qualifications were prescribed for those who wanted to contest. The essential criteria were age limit, possession of immovable property, and minimum educational qualification. Those who wanted to be elected should be above 35 years of age and below 70."

Only those who owned a private property on a private land that attracted taxes and had a minimum educational qualification had the right to contest.

Keshav Mishra

An age limit was applicable (35-70) and the person serving in any committee was not not allowed to contest for the next three terms with each term being of one year.

Overall, democracy and electoral polity were very much similar to the modern system of administration and even slightly better and worse in some terms like minimum educational qualification and owning of private property respectively.

Kautilya or Chanakya (375-283 BCE) was an excellent teacher, author, strategist, philosopher, economist, jurist, and royal advisor. The most insightful aspect of his political belief was what Wolpert termed as 'social-monarchy'. In the first book of Arthshastra, his self-written book, it is stated that a king should be *devoted to the welfare of all beings*. To Chanakya, the center of tenet of *arth* was not only the king and his acquaintances but also the public of the kingdom and topics or issues revolving around it.

Keshav Mishra

According to his ideology, the King and the administrative board should pay attention to children, aged persons, and persons in distress when these are helpless', while the judiciary should look after 'women, minors, old persons, sick persons'.

As the references suggest, there was a municipal board which had one of the many responsibilities, ensuring the employees to get a minimum wage were established. This ensured that the employees weren't violated or taken advantage of by the employer.

Megasthenes' account concurs, noting the moral responsibility felt by Chandragupta (the ruler of the Mauryan empire) towards his subjects.

This sense of responsibility was manifested itself in what Bandhopadhya states as a 'contractual relationship between the king and the people', as Chandragupta strove to not repeat the mistakes of the Nandas in creating distrust and panic.

One great success of Kautilya's policy in general was the emphasis placed on creating direct sessions of communication between ruler and ruled, which made the relationship between the

Keshav Mishra

king and his subjects less antagonistic than it had been under the Nandas.

The direct democratic system of rule can't be found in Chandragupta's time but a near democratic rule was definitely established, people didn't have the power but the King himself was willing to work for the welfare of people according to the requests of people.

Thus, we can see that since the starting of Ancient Indian history till date, India, World's largest democracy had the beliefs and faith in democracy, even in the tyrannic rule of Mughals and Britishers, people voiced themselves in attempt to resurrect the Samjnana of vedic times and it became a reality from a utopia… but is it still a utopia?

Keshav Mishra

CHAPTER - 2

'Democracy is a government of the people, by the people and for the people'

The most famous description of democracy that is circulated worldwide was quoted by Abrahm Lincoln, 16th president of the United States. Democracy, The term has been derived from two Greek words – 'Demos' meaning people and 'Kratos' meaning rule. Literally translated as 'rule of people'. It is such a government where freely elected representatives take administrative decisions.

Practical democracy is a much more advanced and complex term than the theory.
It avails various rights and freedoms to its citizens and asks for the equally precious duty of citizens.

It isn't necessary to get a unanimous favor, democracy works where the majority of the public lies because it's nearly impossible to agree with each and every person.

Keshav Mishra

A successful democracy is where the citizens participate freely in the country, vote to elect leaders, praise the good deeds and criticize the 'mistakes'.

The goal is to elect a leader that really works for the favor of people, according to people, but is that what we get after every five years in India? Do the leaders really work for people instead of making the people work for them? Do they really work according to the people instead of imposing rules in favor of themselves? We will take a wide tour analyzing many famous quotes and again try to answer these questions.

"A functioning, robust democracy requires a healthy, educated, participatory followership, and an educated, morally grounded leadership."

Quoted by Chinua Achebe a Nigerian novelist, poet, and critic who is regarded as a dominant figure in modern African literature. He stated that to achieve a functioning and robust democracy participation of citizens in decision making and electing an *educated* leader who values the morals of fellow humanship.

In other words, if the leadership isn't based on morals, the leader isn't educated or the citizens aren't participating in the

Keshav Mishra

administrative functions or polling then the democracy isn't functioning like what it was meant for.

Taking an example of the chola dynasty mentioned in chapter 1, the rules to elect a new leader clearly stated that one of the conditions to contest elections is having a minimum educational qualifications.

"Everybody counts in applying democracy. And there will never be a true democracy until every responsible and law-abiding adult in it, without regard to race, sex, color or creed has his or her own inalienable and unpurchasable voice in government."

Quoted by Carrie Chapman Catt, a key leader of the American women's suffrage movement. Her oratory and organizational skills led to ratification of the 19th Amendment to the U.S. Constitution granting women the right to vote in August 1920

She says that true democracy will be achieved when every responsible and law-abiding adult will have his **own** voice in government without any regard to race, sex, color or creed. She emphasizes on every adult having his own voice in government that can't be purchased or manipulated by a third person. But is it possible for every responsible citizen to be equally selfless and devoted towards the greater good of the nation? Or even the leaders stay so selfless in front of lucrative selfish benefits? Is selfishness an integral part of humans that we consciously or subconsciously break at a bottom price?

"If you want to raise a crop for one year, plant corn. If you want to raise a crop for decades, plant trees. If you want to raise a crop for centuries, raise men. If you want to plant a crop for eternities, raise democracies."

Carl A Schenck was born in 1868 in the town of Darmstadt, Germany and became a pioneering forestry educator in North America, known for his contributions as the forester for George W. Vanderbilt's Biltmore Estate, and the founder of the Biltmore Forest School, the first practical forestry school in the United States, in 1898, near Brevard, North Carolina

Schenck believes that democracies aren't like other forms of government that come and go as time passes and fade out like an insignificant line in books and logs of history. Democracy is a system which favors people and people will do their best to retain its existence and its nearly impossible to remove it until the

Keshav Mishra

citizens themselves want a dictator to take over due to increase in cons of democracy below a bottom line that may be due to the selfishness of the officials or the lack of participating citizens in administrative or electoral polls, also there may be a chaotic situation where the people are divided into many factions and taking an appropriate decision is difficult leading to introduction of dictatorship but still it will be a win for democracy only. Schenck's views mostly coincide with my own that democracy, once established, is eternal.

"Peace cannot exist without justice, justice cannot exist without fairness, fairness cannot exist without development, development cannot exist without democracy, democracy cannot exist without respect for the identity and worth of cultures and peoples."

Rigoberta Menchú Tum is a K'iche' Guatemalan human rights activist, feminist, and Nobel Peace Prize laureate (1992). Menchú has dedicated her life to publicizing the rights of Guatemala's Indigenous peoples during and after the Guatemalan Civil War (1960–1996), and to promoting Indigenous rights internationally.

Keshav Mishra

His, or in fact every rational human's with moral values ultimate aim lies within peace. He says that justice is essential to achieve peace because in case of injustice, opposition will stand in favor of justice and there will be war between justice and injustice either with weapons or without. To achieve justice, fairness is necessary as only when the judge is sided with fairness along with parties involved, will justice be given, in any case of unfairness, there is a high chance that justice will be transformed into injustice. And fairness cannot exist without development, not just technological but mindset of people, a change in social, economical and cultural development. A mindset free of narrow mindedness, jealousy, greed etc. To achieve development, democracy is needed, an environment where people are the one ruling themselves, not just obeying the orders like slaves, where the people have their own rights and freedom, a place where everyone is equal regardless of their social or economical class, where resources are used for development of mankind rather than filling the pockets of some selfish position holders.

And finally to achieve that utopic place termed as democracy, we need to understand the value of ourselves, the people and our culture, what we are and what we want without any interference of a third party with lucrative offers.

Keshav Mishra

"Man's capacity for justice makes democracy possible, but man's inclination to injustice makes democracy necessary."

Karl Paul Reinhold Niebuhr was an American Reformed theologian, ethicist, commentator on politics and public affairs, and professor at Union Theological Seminary (NY) for more than 30 years. Niebuhr was one of America's leading public intellectuals for several decades of the 20th century and received the Presidential Medal of Freedom in 1964.

My views on this are that a rational man can always or most of the time come to justice if all the aspects of the incident are open to him. That signifies that he holds compassions towards others as a sense of humanity and haves the ability to spare efforts in betterment of his own, the society and mankind by involving in public issues, thus establishing a democracy, but on the other hand, humans are creature with high intelligence, expectation, greed, selfishness etc. and can be easily corrupted. The difference is just that everyone has a different breaking point.

Taking an example, a common peasant may become a slave for a tyrant, that he knows is a tyrant, or even more, don't even know

Keshav Mishra

him, if he can get an irrigation motor from him for his farm. But similarly, if the same offers are given to a multi millionaire, he won't even bat an eyelid for it, to move him, a profit worth millions will be needed.

When the tyranny of dictators becomes indomitable and people get their eyes cleared up due to oppression, they demand their freedom and rights. A life with dignity becomes a luxury only a few can afford and people finally stand against them to get back what belongs to them, their freedom and dignity, a necessity to live for a human. Thus democracy becomes necessary.

"If we want to cultivate a true spirit of democracy we cannot afford to be intolerant. Intolerance betrays want of faith in one's cause"

Mahatma Gandhi quotes the above lines. He emphasized on how public opinion and participation in administrative affairs helps in building the foundation of democracy. Especially criticizing and not tolerating any injustice or wrongdoing of the current government. If the elected representative is left untouched even after an injustice or wrong decision, the public's faith over

Keshav Mishra

democratic rights and qualities will waver that may lead to total loss of democracy and start of a new and dark era.

"In coming years, we've to focus on 'Panchpran'- First, to move forward with bigger resolves & resolve of developed India; Second, erase all traces of servitude; Third, be proud of our legacy; Fourth, strength of unity and Fifth, duties of citizens which includes the Prime Minister and Chief Ministers."

The current Prime Minister, Narendra Modi addressed the nation with these lines on 75 years of Independence. He mentioned at last of the lines about the importance of duties of citizens that not only the common people but also those in position have to exercise. One of the points of duties of citizens as mentioned in the constitution of India says to develop a spirit of inquiry and reform. An individual must exercise this and question his confusion to the authorities and criticize the same if he finds that the fundamentals of justice, constitution or humanity are threatened. A state may not realize the the true value of the currently elected leader until a new leader is appointed to bring a change, only a change may show the true level of administration in different hands, of course the decision to elect a representative

Keshav Mishra

finally lands in the hands of public only if they really know the true capability of all volunteers.

There may be some differences in opinions but all the leaders have the same aim towards democracy, that is, participation of citizens in administrative affairs to keep the representatives in check and justice and duties of citizens.

But is it really possible to create a place where everyone is participating, standing against injustice, selfless, willing to promote righteousness? We will have a walkthrough around a hypocritical world, where every quality, that we think is necessary in democracy will be present and analyze if that world can only exist in utopia or can come to reality?

Keshav Mishra

CHAPTER - 3

(Note : Chapter 3 is a fictional world which shows how an ideal democracy can fall because of absence of what we think of as a monster in democracy. Further examples will be taken from this chapter.)

Taking a quick shower, Aryan hurried towards his wardrobe to dress up. A man in his early twenties with a wide grin and gleaming eyes dressed in formals with a brown leather handbag was reflected in the wardrobe mirror.

'Finally! A day which each and every citizen of India was waiting for has come to our doorstep. Thanks to the freedom fighters and brave men' thought Aryan while eating Aloo Paratha in his breakfast which tasted like never before because it was his first meal of freedom.

"Public party *zindabad*!"

"Public party *zindabad*!"

"Public party *zindabad*!"

Keshav Mishra

After exiting his two story tall, decent home and stepping into the busy streets of Lucknow, he saw waves and waves of people carrying huge banners and flags of purple color and shouting to show their favor towards the public party. It was an enjoyment for him to see people rallying without any fear of oppression by the British officials.

After traveling for half an hour by foot, he reached his office with wrinkles of happiness on his shirt and dirt of freedom in his hair which was ten minutes from his home.

"Hey Aryan! Hurry over! Today is the most awaited election day, the first election day of Independent India! We must hurry up and leave with the crew for the opinions of people" Sultan's voice rang in his ears and he jolted out from his own fantasies. Sultan was his colleague and cameraman, a 24 year old guy with a ruddy complexion.

"Sure, let's gather the crew and equipment and to exercise our freedom, media's freedom and India's freedom."

"Let's go!"

Keshav Mishra

After approximately 15 minutes, a typical white van with a big logo in blue and red and a dish antenna at the top exited the garage of a multi story and under construction building of India's most flourishing media company.

"Where should we go first?" Sultan asked.

"Let's steer to Aminabad, there is always a massive crowd there, we'll be able to review many people there." Aryan replied

"As you wish my lord!" Sultan laughed like a maniac.

…

"Today is one of the most memorable days in history, may I know your views for it?" Standing in front of his cameraman, Aryan spoke with great confidence, asking a group of youths waiting for their turn to vote in front the polling booth.

"This year, 1951, will be engraved in Indian history and we are extremely ecstatic at the thought that we are going to be a part of it. I'm here to support the People's party, because it gave a statement where the board members thoroughly mentioned how they'll work on construction of roads in every village in India in the next five years. Furthermore, they favored financially supporting the families of freedom fighters and promised to thoroughly work on promoting handloom workers."

"I'm a taxi driver and I'll support the democratic party as it has a great past record. The current members of the party in the past helped many people during the natural calamities. It promised during the last press release that it will spread great influence in cleanliness which will lead to lesser risk of diseases for people."
…
"The Public party introduced an import and export scheme that will significantly boost the economy of the country".

…

A similar review was taken by multitudes of media firms and was displayed live on the television. In front of the television sat an old man with strong posture and intimidating aura. He wore black hoodie and his face was covered in a veil of darkness. His eyes shone like blood moons by the reflection of T V. A shrill and frightening laughter rang throughout the area but unfortunately, only crows resided there to witness the birth of…

Keshav Mishra

…

After 4 months…

Aryan was reading headlines while sitting on the comfortable seat in his office. According to the newspaper, the People's party won the election, the same party which offered quality education, promoting handloom workers, constructing roads in villages etc.

The reports said that there was 100 per cent participation of people and no party was able to establish a dominating majority thus, a collective government was formed by six parties under the lead of People's party. Furthermore due to too much of a crowd in a few places, many skirmishes sprang up in view of conflicting thoughts of people. In the name of freedom, people took the constitution in their hands and the situation was out of control of the police force for a few hours. After 4 hours of hard work, the situation finally came under control.

"Today is one of the most memorable days in history, may I know your views for it?" The same question was repeated by Aryan in front of a crowd of women in Hazratganj.

Keshav Mishra

"The People's party will be a better choice according to me because it promised to promote feasible and standard education at government institutions."

Many similar reports were listed one after another, a few hundred of theft by taking advantage of the crowd and a few hundred of theft at empty houses. There were as many as 34 listed casualties throughout the country.

Furthermore, the four months of administration without a leader was chaotic, Indian economy fell like a ball thrown from a bridge, international boundaries were threatened, refugees coming from pakistan and East pakistan (Bangladesh) were scorned and didn't had a place to stay, many instances were where the executives were confused by getting orders of differing opinions.

The judiciary was having difficulty in announcing a justice in cases of unavailability of direct evidence due to differing opinions and criticisms of the public.

sigh "I never expected that active participation of the public in administrative issues would lead to such cases. Anyways, what's done is done, I hope that now a government is formed, everything

Keshav Mishra

will settle down and a new era of India will begin. The positive thing is that we don't have corruption here and all the officials are in high spirits of freedom, I guess they won't be corrupted… at least I hope so." blabbered Aryan matter of factly with a sour expression and three lined frown on his glabella.

"Same do I" commented Sultan "They say that a democracy is successful when the people have an active participation and say in public affairs, but I never thought that this is what we know as an ideal democracy."

…

After two years (1953)…

In parliament, the prime minister said enthusiastically "We need to take up steps to enhance and stabilize India's economy to get a hold and say on international platforms. To do that we must provide benefits and resources to farmers to increase agricultural productivity. Secondly, we need to focus on industries….."

…

Keshav Mishra

After two years (1955)

In parliament, the prime minister said with a stiff posture and frustrated look "I would like to remind you all that we need to boost up the Indian economy and to get it done…"

"But to pass the bill we need the opinion of people of our constituencies and they are not expressing a single viewpoint, we should wait till they have made up their mind, this is a democratic assembly after all, how can we jump to the conclusions if the people don't agree" A plump minister stood up the Prime Minister's proposal and stated a point which most of the MLA's agreed to.

…

After two years (1967)

Standing on a wooden stage in Delhi, the retired Prime Minister addressed the crowd "The Indian economy is constantly falling, we need to pay serious attention to this fact…"

…

Keshav Mishra

In the outer region of Lucknow, 29 kilometers east of the capital is a barren and shady region. An old man sat on a creaking chair and wrote down about the unsuccessful attempts of the old prime minister in his black diary with yellowish pages. The wind blew through the half open window of the single story house beside a crooked leafless tree that looked as if it could fall any time. The pages of creepy diary blew and daily political events of the last six years! Especially, about how people are corruption free and no one attempts or accepts corruption as if people don't know that a thing like corruption even exists!

"My time has come…HaHaHaHa…!" again only crows danced at the shrill laughter under the crescent moon which looked darker than the night of the new moon.

…

A police officer took 2000 rupees from an Old man to let him go after breaking traffic rules.

…

A district level competition organizer took 15000 rupees from an old man to make him win 30000 rupees worth scholarship.

Keshav Mishra

…

After four years…

Aryan and Sultan took their van to visit a polling booth in a village. After reaching a crowded area, they approached a group of farmers and asked.

"What are your opinions for these elections?"

And swiftly came a reply "We all are in support of Republic Party of India"

A wide grin was etched on the face of Aryan. He thought 'these people are really active, even after the craze of elections are gone they are so adamant about supporting RPI.'

"Why do you support them? There must be something they have done to make you all support them." He asked in an enthusiastic manner.

"We all got a bottle full of kerosene oil!"

Keshav Mishra

…

On the result day…

Aryan said almost helplessly "I would never have hoped to see an India with corruption, I…"

"Don't you think there is something weird about how all the people are only bribed and corrupted by RPI? I guess we didn't got a single report where people were bribed by any other party to achieve their goals." Sultan exclaimed as he suddenly jumped from his chair and interrupted Aryan.
"What do you mean?" asked Aryan while tilting his head in confusion.

"A scary thought just came to my mind. If what I think is true then a democracy can't exist without corruption." Sultan said in a nearly inaudible voice while having cold sweat dripping from his back.

Before he could explain any further, the news reporter mentioned the winning of RPI and Sultan fainted!

Keshav Mishra

...

After 2 months

At a public square in Delhi, the new prime minister came forward to address the people of the Republic of India. He was an old man with a strong posture and a pair of intimidating eyes, he had a face that spoke volumes about his western genes. After his long and boring speech he said "Hence from today onwards, I, Micheal will be the sole dictator of India!". Surprisingly, instead of opposition people cheered up in favor. They were bought and corrupted over by a sole corrupter.

> *'Venom is a must to a snake,*
> *Extreme heat composes the sun,*
> *Millenniums of pressure produces a diamond,*
> *Even corruption is the stabilizer for democracy!'*

We will talk about how democracy fails if we put all the theories and ideals into practical use by analyzing the above example.

Keshav Mishra

<u>Bibliography and References</u>

<u>Ramcharitmanas</u>

<u>Arthashastra</u>

<u>https://www.gktoday.in/topic/sabha-and-samiti-in-vedic-civilization/</u>

<u>https://www.sacred-texts.com/hin/rvsan/rv10191.htm</u>

<u>https://www.booksfact.com/vedas/rig-veda/ancient-democracy-in-vedas-buddhist-greek-history.html</u>

<u>https://www.tribuneindia.com/news/archive/features/democracy-has-roots-in-harappa-233774</u>

<u>https://www.thehindu.com/news/national/tamil-nadu/Uttaramerur-model-of-democracy/article16566830.ece</u>

<u>https://www.wikipedia.org/</u>

<u>https://www.mkgandhi.org/</u>

Keshav Mishra

https://www.thehindubusinessline.com/

http://youngindia.gov.in/

https://www.ipu.org/news/news-in-brief/2021-09/you-may-not-know-these-7-quotes-democracy

Keshav Mishra